THE CELL CYCLE

JOSEPH MIDTHUN   SAMUEL HITI

BUILDING BLOCKS
SCIENCE

WORLD BOOK

www.worldbook.com

World Book, Inc.
180 North LaSalle Street
Suite 900
Chicago, Illinois 60601
USA

For information about other World Book publications,
visit our website at www.worldbook.com
or call 1-800-WORLDBK (967-5325).
For information about sales to schools and libraries,
call 1-800-975-3250 (United States),
or 1-800-837-5365 (Canada).

Building Blocks of Science:
  The Cell Cycle
ISBN: 978-0-7166-7879-3 (trade, hc.)
ISBN: 978-0-7166-7887-8 (pbk.)
ISBN: 978-0-7166-2962-7 (e-book, EPUB3)

Acknowledgments:
Created by Samuel Hiti and Joseph Midthun
Art by Samuel Hiti
Text by Joseph Midthun
Special thanks to Syril McNally

TABLE OF CONTENTS

There is a glossary on page 30. Terms defined in the glossary are in type **that looks like this** on their first appearance.

CELLS

Plants and animals are living things—

Organisms!

The bodies of all organisms are made of much tinier units called—

I'm an animal cell!

Cells!

I'm a plant cell!

You could say that a cell is the building block of life.

Cells work together to make up all of the organisms on Earth...

...but at first glance, it can be hard to tell.

You need a microscope to see most cells and their tiny world.

Some living things are made up of only one tiny cell. But, many organisms, like this flower, are made up of millions of cells!

Wow! Cells like me make up this flower!

On the other hand, the human body has more than 10 trillion (10,000,000,000,000) cells!

You can see many differences between the cells of plants and animals.

munch munch

Yet, plant and animal cells also share some major similarities.

Let's take a closer look!

REGULATING LIFE CYCLES

Just like other organisms, cells pass through stages called a **life cycle** as they grow and develop.

Life cycles help us understand how living things change over time.

Even as an adult, the cells inside your body will continue to divide and guide your life cycle.

And, like most organisms, the life cycle of the cell includes death.

Each day, several billion cells in the body die—

—and are replaced.

Piff

In the time that it takes you to read this sentence, millions of your skin cells will have died and been replaced.

Dead cells from internal **organs** pass out of the body with waste.

Most white blood cells live about 13 days, while red blood cells live about 120 days.

Nerve cells might live up to 100 years.

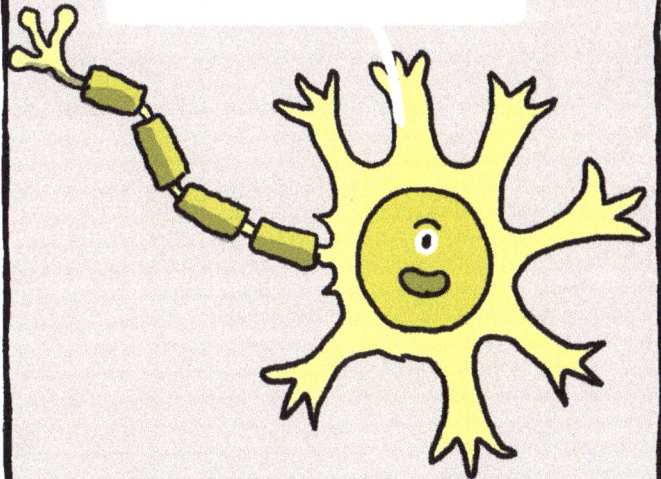

In the plant kingdom, death is somewhat different.

Sometimes, plant cells seem to live until they are no longer needed by the plant.

However, if this flower doesn't get enough water...

...entire **structures**, like leaves, or even the stem, can wither and die.

Flop

7

PARTS OF THE CELL

Like all other organisms, all cells have their own life cycles.

They grow, use energy, get rid of wastes, and even die.

Both plant and animal cells have a thin covering called the **cell membrane.**

ANIMAL CELL

CHROMOSOME

NUCLEUS

VACUOLE

CYTOPLASM

MITOCHONDRIA

CELL MEMBRANE

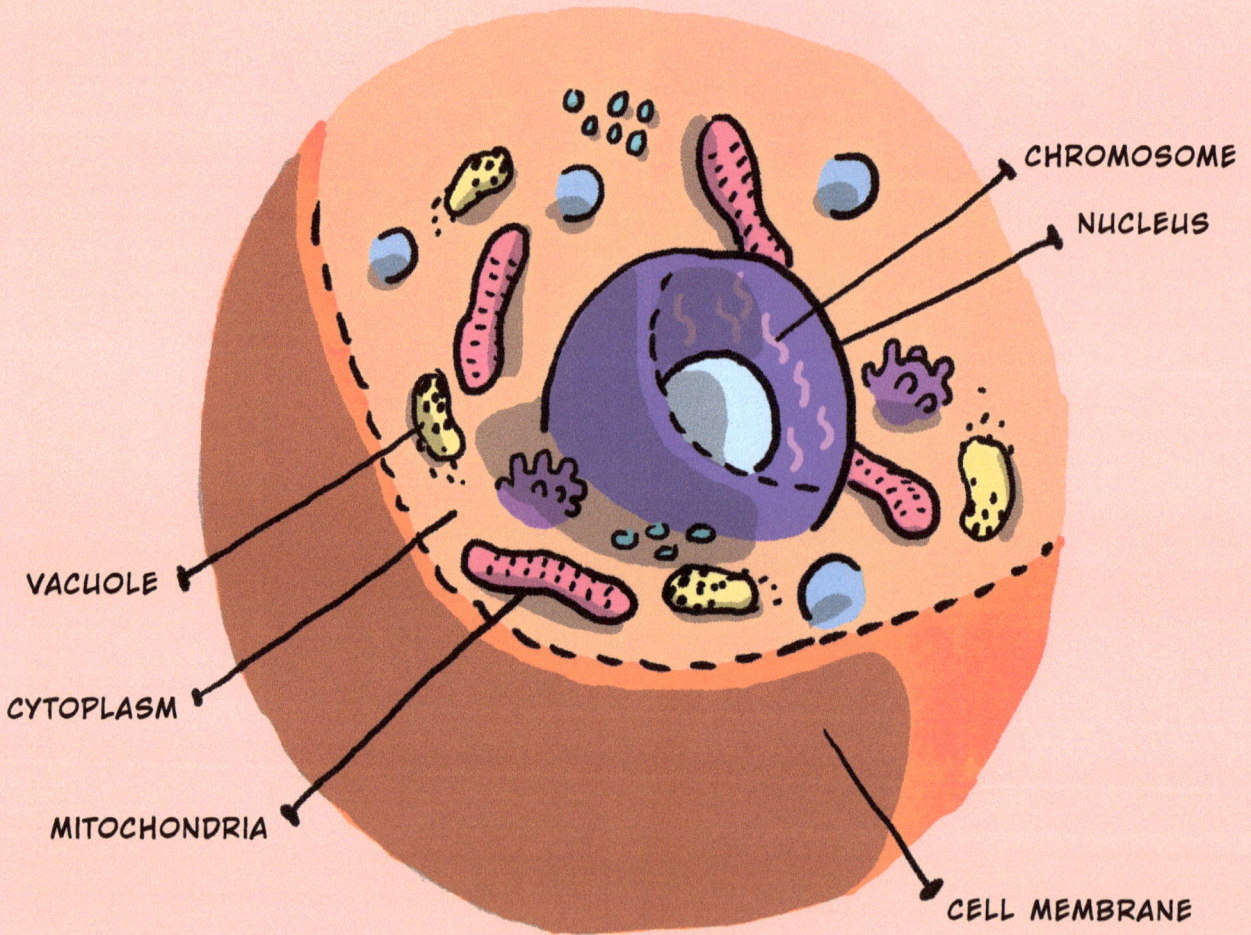

A cell membrane is kind of a "skin" that covers the cell's insides and keeps it all together.

Just as your skin separates you from your surroundings, this membrane separates individual cells from each other.

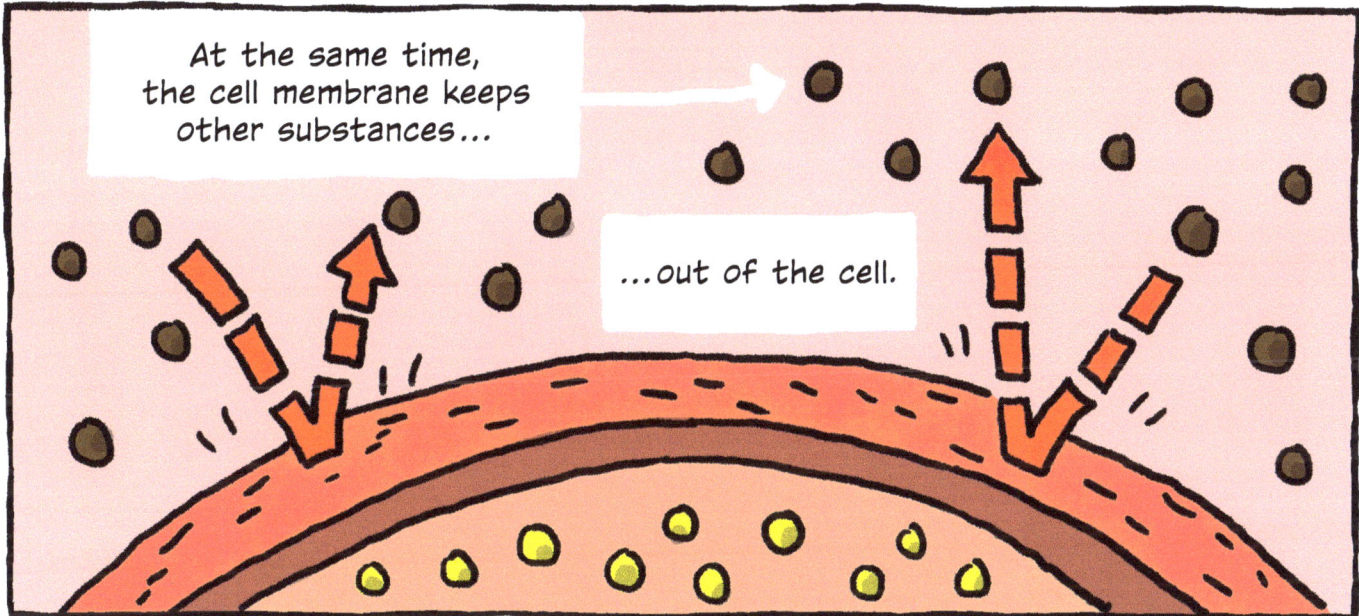

All the basic functions for life take place inside the cell membrane.

All cells have structures that perform different tasks.

Both plant and animal cells have a jellylike substance, called **cytoplasm**, that fills the inside of the cell.

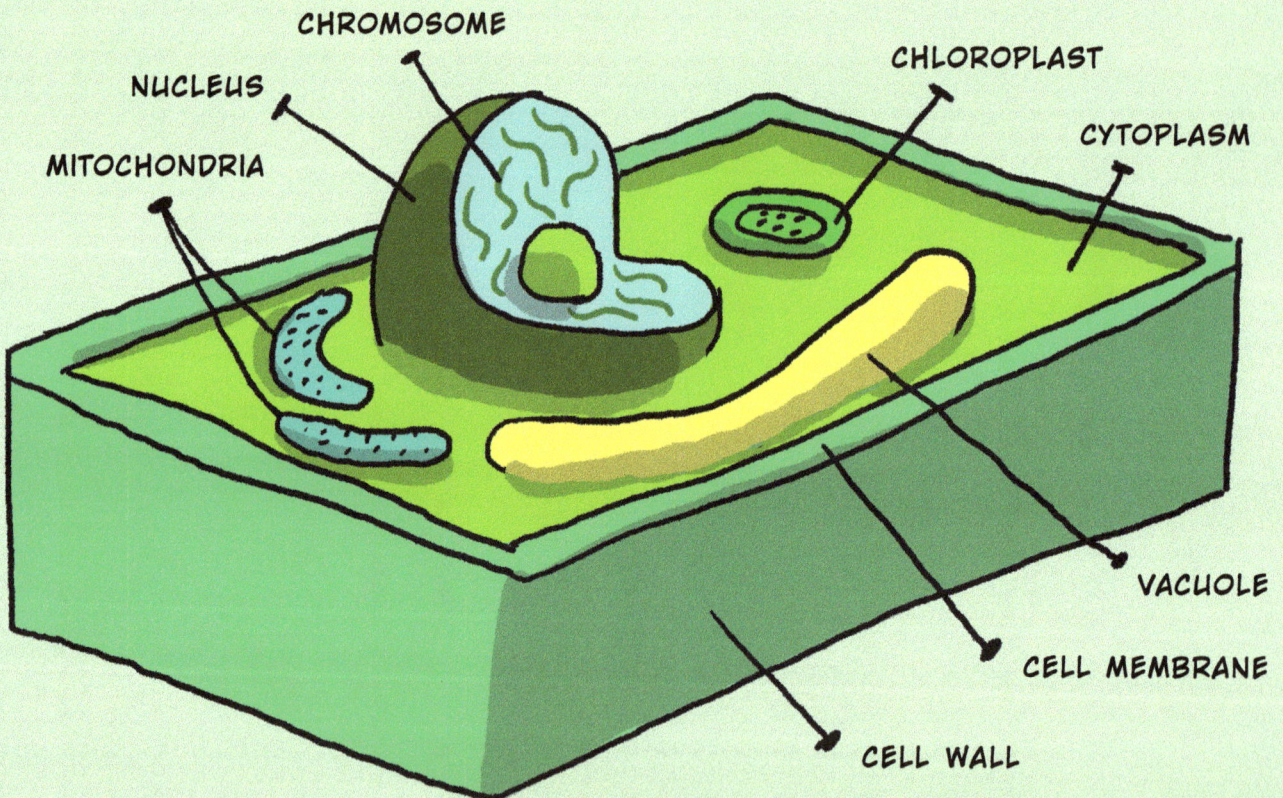

PLANT CELL

CHROMOSOME

NUCLEUS

MITOCHONDRIA

CHLOROPLAST

CYTOPLASM

VACUOLE

CELL MEMBRANE

CELL WALL

The cytoplasm holds all of the materials needed for the cell to perform its activities, such as growth and repair.

It also houses the internal structures that make up the cell...

...the **organelles.**

Plant and animal cells both use energy from food to live.

Inside a cell, food is turned into energy by organelles called **mitochondria.**

The mitochondria are the power plants of the cell.

Chemical reactions inside these organelles transform food into energy.

The cell can then use the energy to perform different life functions, such as getting rid of wastes.

Cells use energy to work together to perform important functions—

pant pant

—like breathing!

Cells also have internal structures called **vacuoles.**

These fluid-filled vacuoles store the cell's food, water, and waste materials.

The materials stored in vacuoles can be used by the cell...

...or discarded by the cell.

Both plant cells and animal cells have vacuoles.

However, while animal cells may have many small vacuoles, plant cells usually have only one or two big vacuoles.

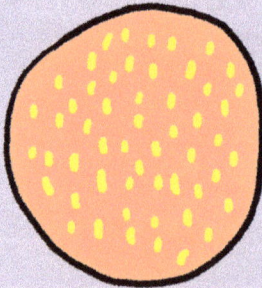

Plant and animal cells both have a "control center" called the **nucleus.**

The nucleus directs all of the activities of the cell.

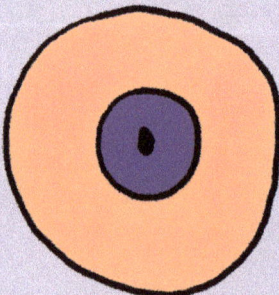

Inside of the nucleus are the cell's **chromosomes.**

Chromosomes are long, threadlike strands...

KICK

...patterns of **DNA** that control how a cell grows, develops, and does its job.

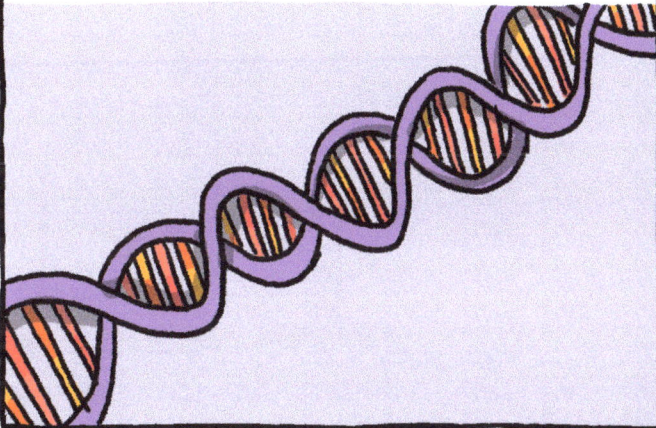

These chromosomes exist in pairs, and they help produce all the different substances that make up the cell.

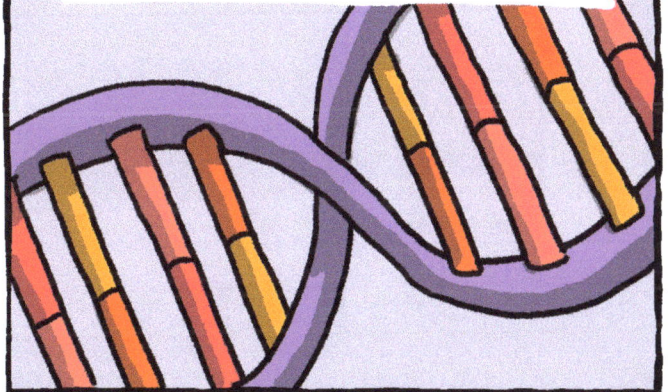

Your patterns of DNA are the product of half of your mother's chromosomes combined with half of your father's chromosomes.

Every species of life has a certain number of chromosomes in each of its body's cells.

But, remember, for all the similarities between their cells, you can usually tell by looking at them that...

First, plant cells have some structures that animal cells do not.

These structures can help us tell the difference between plant and animal cells.

...animal cells and plant cells are not exactly the same.

Plant cells have important differences from animal cells.

Parts of the Cell	Animal Cells	Plant Cells
Cell membrane	✓	✓
Cell wall		✓
Chloroplasts		✓
Chromosomes	✓	✓
Cytoplasm	✓	✓
Mitochondria	✓	✓
Nucleus	✓	✓
Vacuole	many small	few large

While most animal cells usually have a round shape, all plant cells have an additional stiff covering outside the cell membrane called—

—the cell wall!

WHOA!

The cell wall is the feature that gives plant cells a squarelike shape.

Cool!

Millions of these cell walls work together to give plant branches the strength to hold up a leaf.

And billions of cell walls together give tree trunks the sturdiness to hold up hundreds, even thousands of leaves.

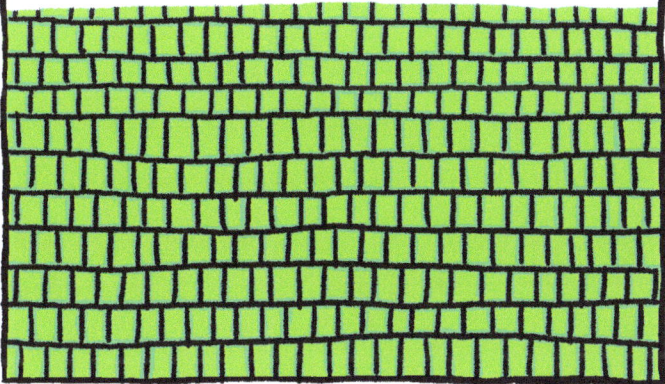

So, if you see that a cell has a boxy shape and a surrounding cell wall, it is most likely a plant cell.

Another feature found in plant cells, but not animal cells, is the **chloroplast.**

Chloroplasts are filled with a green substance called **chlorophyll.**

Chloroplasts are the "food factories" for plants, and the chlorophyll inside of them gives plants their green color.

Through a process called **photosynthesis,** chloroplasts in each cell produce food from water and other materials by using energy from sunlight.

The energy from sunlight causes a water molecule to split apart inside the chloroplasts, separating its hydrogen and oxygen **atoms.**

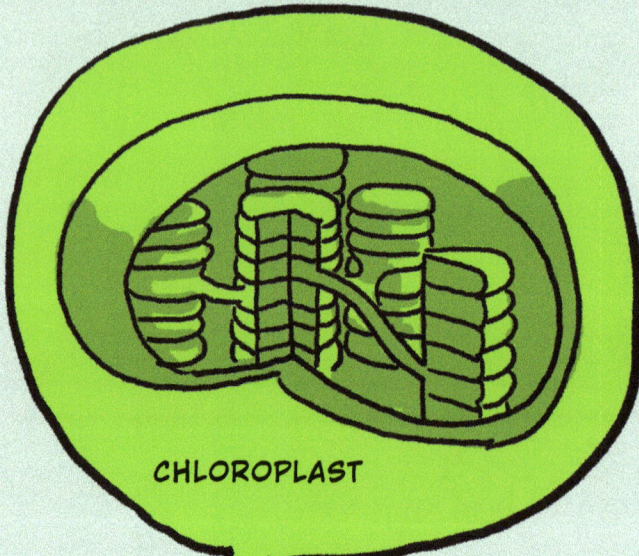

CHLOROPLAST

In a series of complicated steps, the hydrogen combines with carbon dioxide from the air to form a simple sugar inside the plant.

The oxygen from the water is released back into the environment.

From these sugars, and other nutrients from the soil, plants can make starch, fat, protein, and vitamins that are needed for life.

Photosynthesis provides the energy needed to make enough food for the whole plant to use!

Animal cells do not have chloroplasts or chlorophyll.

So, if you notice that a cell is green in color, it is most likely a plant cell.

CELL DIVISION

Like other living things, cells **reproduce,** and they do it in a spectacular way.

Every living thing is made up of one or more cells.

Each of these cells was made from an already existing cell.

New cells are produced in a process called **cell division.**

Cell division, or splitting, creates two cells where there was once only one cell.

Plop

Single-celled organisms begin and complete their lives as single cells.

Human beings and other multicellular organisms also develop from a single cell.

After the cell grows to a certain size, it divides and forms two cells.

These two cells remain attached to each other.

Plop

They grow and divide, forming four cells.

plop   Plop

The cells grow and divide over and over again, and during this process, they begin to work together in the body as such structures as tissues and organs.

plop plop   plop plop

Cell division happens throughout an organism's entire life.

Cell division involves many processes.

Plop

In the first process, called **nuclear division**, the chromosomes are copied and the nucleus divides.

The next process is called **cytokinesis**, where the cytoplasm divides and creates two new cells.

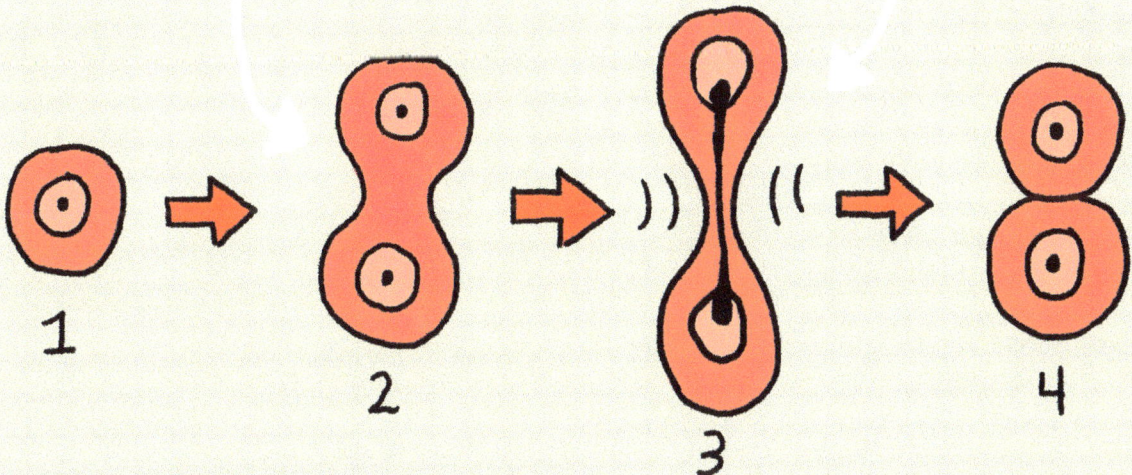

1   2   3   4

MITOSIS

There are two types of nuclear division...

...**mitosis** and **meiosis**.

I'm ready to divide!

Most cells divide their nucleus through mitosis.

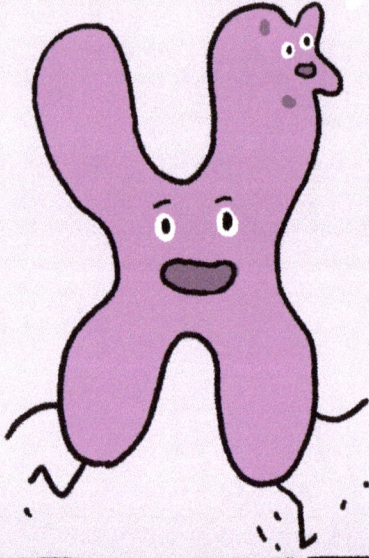

In this process, the chromosomes first make copies of themselves, and then the nucleus divides inside the cell to form two identical **nuclei.**

Mitosis takes place in four stages...

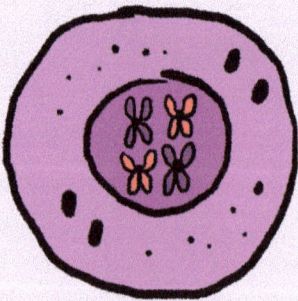

...prophase...

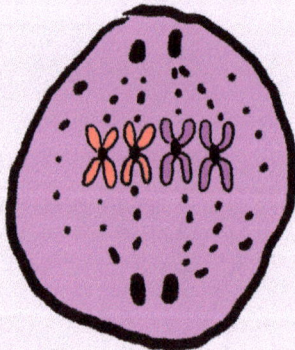

...metaphase...

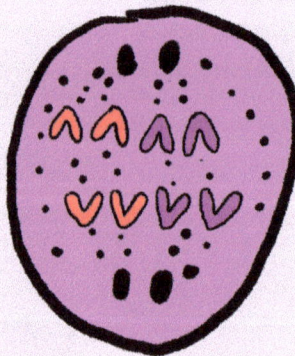

...anaphase...

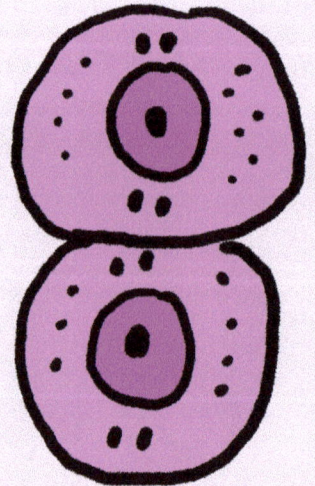

...and telophase.

At the end of telophase, the two new **daughter cells** split through a process called cytokinesis, and mitosis is complete!

The time between the completion of one mitosis division and the beginning of the next is called interphase.

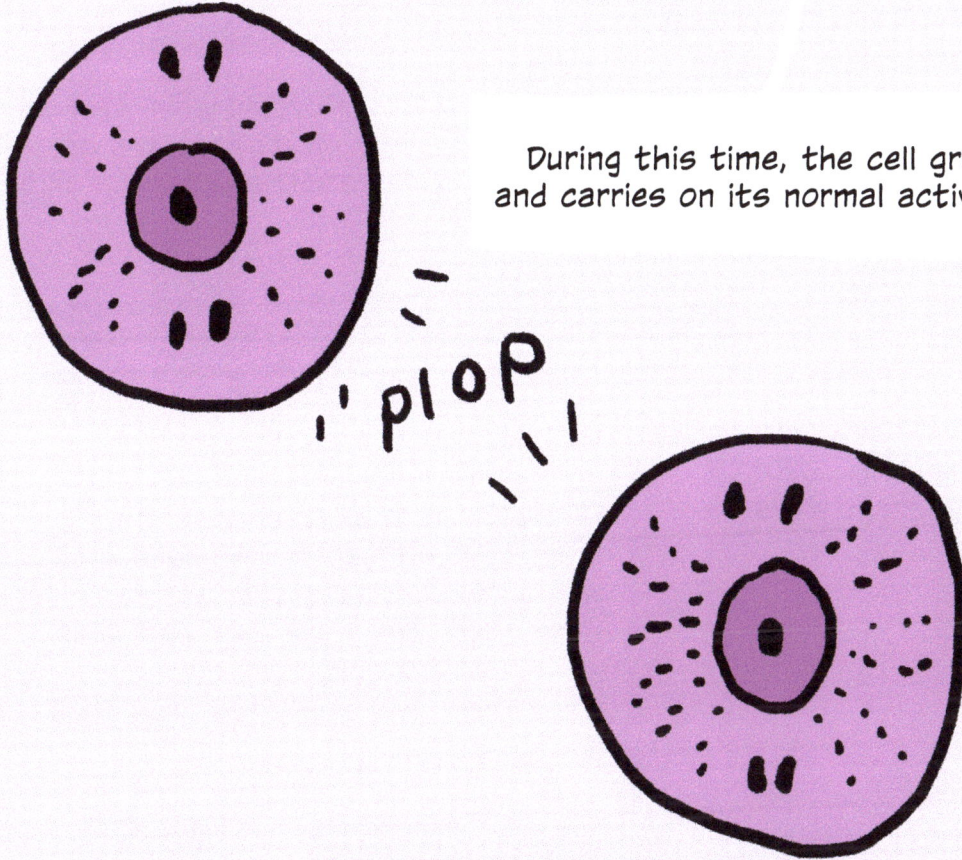

During this time, the cell grows and carries on its normal activities.

plop

Each chromosome makes a copy of itself at a particular time during interphase.

After copying the chromosomes, the cell is ready to undergo mitosis once again.

Plop

In the last stage of mitosis in animal cells, the cytoplasm divides to create two new daughter cells with identical nuclei.

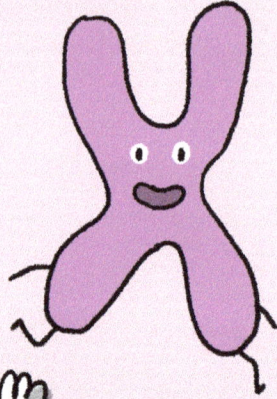

This is called cytokinesis.

After cytokinesis, the cells go into interphase and get ready for another round of mitosis!

In plant cells, both mitosis and cytokinesis occur, but in different ways.

One main difference is that during plant cell cytokinesis, a cell wall grows between the two daughter nuclei to form the two new cells.

CELL WALL

INTERPHASE   PROPHASE   METAPHASE   ANAPHASE   TELOPHASE

After cytokinesis and mitosis are complete, the new cells should have the same number of chromosomes as the original cell and have the same pattern of DNA.

However, cytokinesis does not always create two identical cells—

—this is one time when some mistakes can happen that affect cell growth.

PIOP

Sometimes, one of the daughter cells receives more of one kind of organelle than the other cell.

Hey!

Cytokinesis may also make two different-sized cells.

PIOP

What's the big idea?!

In addition, if mitosis happens more than once in the same cell without cytokinesis, the cell may have more than one nucleus!

Yep! I've got two of 'em!

Another type of nuclear division is called meiosis.

Some organisms can reproduce **sexually.**

This process involves sex cells, also called **gametes,** made in separate reproductive organs.

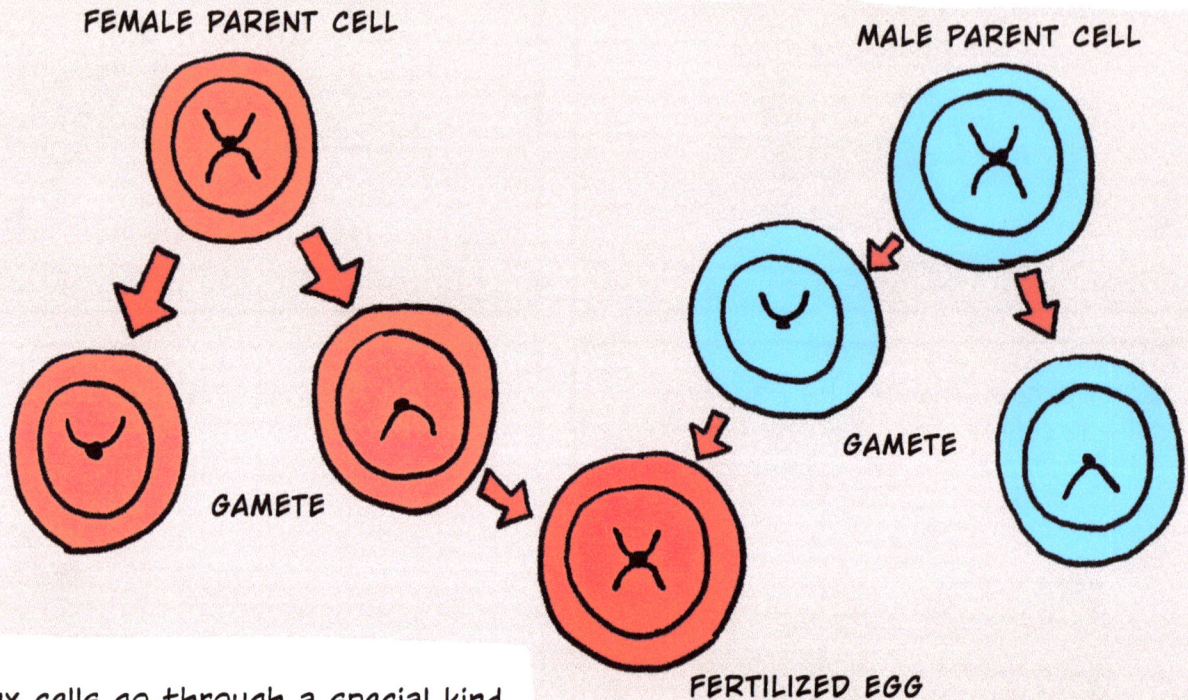

FEMALE PARENT CELL

MALE PARENT CELL

GAMETE

GAMETE

FERTILIZED EGG

Sex cells go through a special kind of cell division called meiosis.

In meiosis, the pairs of chromosomes split up and cells divide.

But, when sex cells divide, the new cells have only half of the number of chromosomes than the other body cells.

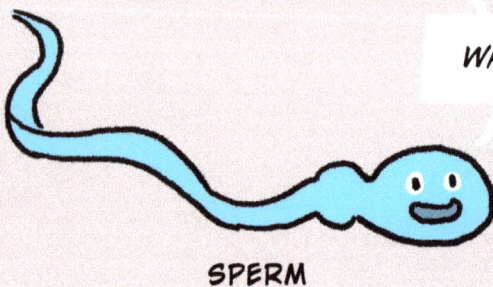

Why?

SPERM

A new individual can be created only if a male sex cell, called a **sperm,** unites with a female sex cell, called an **egg.**

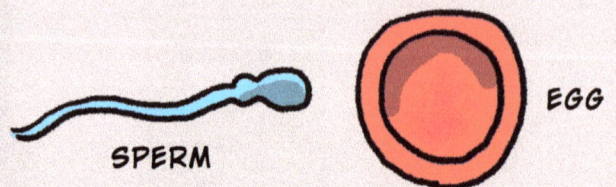

SPERM

EGG

This is called **fertilization.**

When a human sperm fertilizes a human egg, they produce a single cell that combines each sex cell's chromosomes—

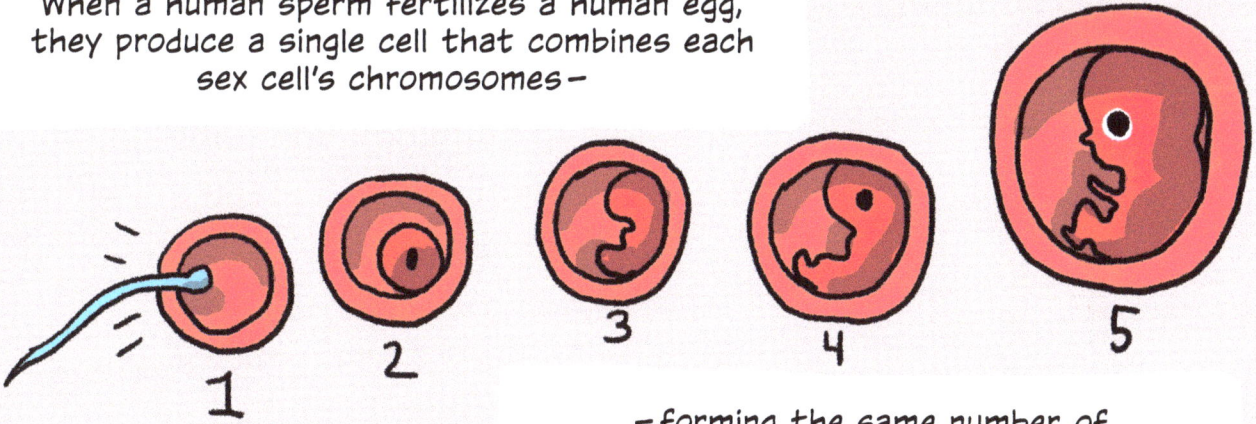

1 2 3 4 5

—forming the same number of chromosomes as the rest of the body cells!

Human beings have 46 total chromosomes, or 23 similar pairs.

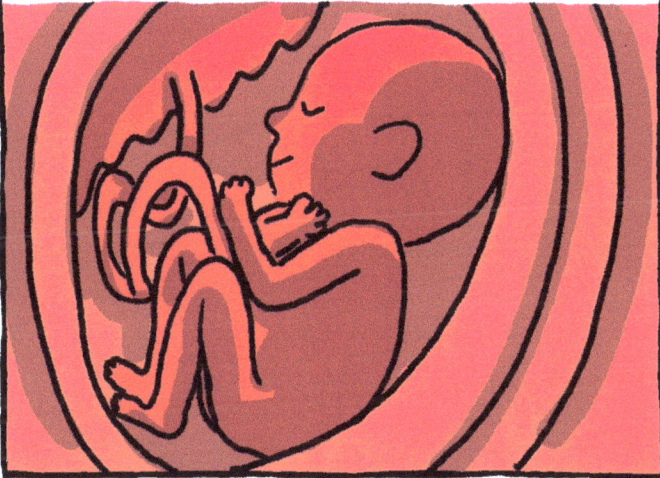

Frogs have 13 pairs, and pea plants have 7 pairs.

The fertilized egg takes its complete set of chromosomes—

—some from the father and some from the mother—

—and continues to develop a new organism.

HOP

DISEASE

Sometimes things go wrong, even for cells.

Instead of dividing in an orderly fashion, a cell may go wild and multiply without stopping...

...or, a **virus** may take over the cell for its own purposes...

...destroying the cell in the process and making the organism sick.

Cancer is a disease marked by an out-of-control growth of cells, called a **tumor**.

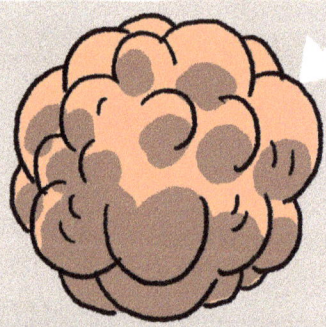

This disease occurs in human beings and other animals.

Many cancer cells look like young cells that have not yet developed.

In some cancerous tissues, many nuclei are in the process of mitosis.

But mitosis never finished and the dividing cells pile up to form a tumor.

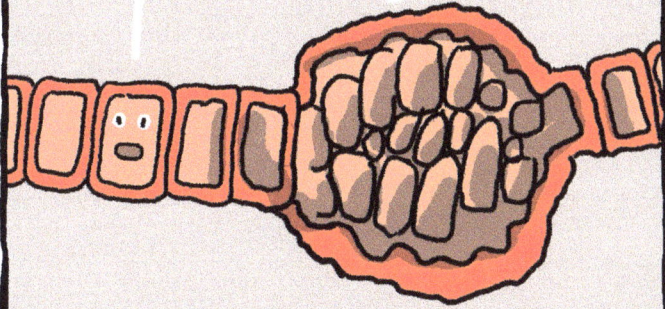

Cells in the tumor may break away, invade other tissues, and form more tumors that disrupt the function of the tissue.

Disease can also come when a tiny virus invades a cell.

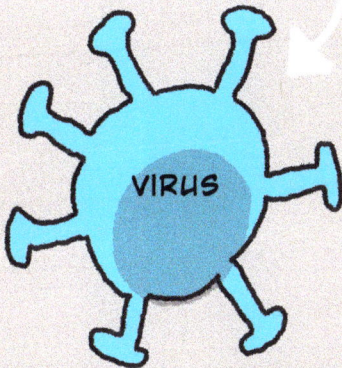

VIRUS

By themselves, viruses are lifeless...

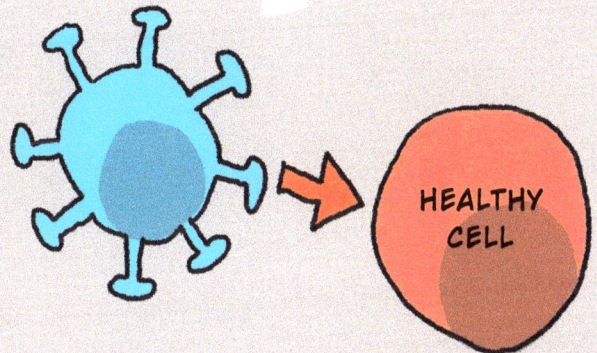

HEALTHY CELL

...but once inside a living cell, viruses become active and take over the cell's controls to make many more copies of themselves.

crash

If not stopped, the new viruses go on to infect other cells.

Makes you wonder if you should start to watch your step!

HOP.

After all, your life cycle is made up of how many cell life cycles?!

Take a minute to try to figure out how many cell life cycles it has taken to read this book!

It's too many to count!

Let's face it, if it weren't for your cells, you just wouldn't be you.

And all living things are made of cells.

HOP

GLOSSARY

atom the basic unit of matter.

cancer a disease marked by an out-of-control growth of body cells.

cell the basic unit of all living things.

cell division the process by which cells split and make new cells.

cell membrane a covering that separates the inside of a cell from the outside environment.

cell wall the stiff covering outside of the cell membrane in a plant cell.

chlorophyll the green pigment in plant cells that helps with photosynthesis.

chloroplast the "food factory" in a plant cell.

chromosomes tiny threadlike strands that carry genes.

cytokinesis a process of cell division in which the cytoplasm divides to make two new cells.

cytoplasm the material that fills a cell.

daughter cells the new cells formed as a result of cell division.

DNA the chainlike structures found in cells that direct cell formation and growth.

egg the female reproductive cell.

fertilization the process by which a male sperm cell and a female egg cell join together.

gametes an organism's sex cells.

life cycle the stages that a living thing goes through as it develops.

meiosis a special type of cell division in sex cells.

mitochondria the "power plants" of a cell.

mitosis the process by which the nucleus divides and forms two identical nuclei in two new cells.

nuclear division a process of cell division in which the nucleus divides.

nucleus; nuclei the "control center" of a cell; more than one nucleus.

organ a special group of cells that work together to help the body function.

organelle a structure within the cell that has a specific job.

organism any living thing.

photosynthesis the process by which plants make their own food.

reproduce the way living things make more of their own kind.

sexual reproduction the process by which organisms produce offspring with sperm cells and egg cells.

sperm the male reproductive cell.

structure a body part of a living thing.

tumor an abnormal buildup and growth of cells on a body part.

vacuole a storage space in a cell.

virus a tiny substance that causes certain illnesses.

FIND OUT MORE

Books

All About Mitosis and Meiosis
by Elizabeth R. Mankato Cregan
(Compass Point, 2010)

Cell
by Richard Spilsbury and
Louise Spilsbury
(Heinemann Library, 2014)

Cell Biology
by Aubrey Stimola
(Rosen Central, 2011)

Cells
by Susan Meredith
(Rourke, 2010)

Cells Up Close
by Maria Nelson
(Gareth Stevens, 2014)

Inheritance and Reproduction
by Jen Green
(Capstone Heinemann Library, 2014)

The Manga Guide to Biochemistry
by Takemura, Masaharu, and Kikuyar
(No Starch Press, 2011)

Websites

BBC Bitesize Science: What's in a Cell?
http://www.bbc.co.uk/schools
/gcsebitesize/science/add_edexcel
/cells/cells1.shtml
The structures, features, and
functions of cells are examined in a
short unit, complete with diagrams
and boldface key terms.

BBC Bitesize Science: Mitosis and Meiosis
http://www.bbc.co.uk/schools
/gcsebitesize/science/add_edexcel/cells
/mitosisact.shtml
Find out why cell division is so important
during reproduction in this narrated
activity.

BBC Bitesize Science: Cells to Systems
http://www.bbc.co.uk/bitesize/ks3
/science/organisms_behaviour_health
/cells_systems/revision/1/
Read about plant and animal cell functions
and then complete an animated instruc-
tional video and a multiple-choice test.

Centre of the Cell: All About Cells
http://www.centreofthecell.org
/centre/?page_id=1&ks=2
Take an in-depth look at animal cells and
examine the life inside your cells.

Centre of the Cell: Games and Interactives
http://www.centreofthecell.org/games/
Select a topic to play a clickable game,
or explore a 3D cell model to learn more
about their function in your body.

Nobelprize.org: Control of the Cell Cycle
http://www.nobelprize.org/educational
/medicine/2001/cellcycle.html
Become a Cell Division Supervisor as you
enter the nucleus and guide the cell
through the phases of cell division.

Nova Online: How Cells Divide
http://www.pbs.org/wgbh/nova/body
/how-cells-divide.html
Travel into the tiny world of cells and
explore cell division with interactive,
animated diagrams.

PBS LearningMedia: Cell Division
http://www.pbslearningmedia.org
/resource/lsps07.sci.life.stru.celldivision
/cell-division/
Learn why cells are critical to life on
Earth in this step-by-step examination
of cell division, with bonus discussion
questions.

INDEX

www.ingramcontent.com/pod-product-compliance
Lightning Source LLC
LaVergne TN
LVHW070840080426
835513LV00023B/2421